The Spider's Web

A tale of interwoven families
and a sequel to
There's One Born Every Minute

A. W. Cullimore

This book was designed
and published in 2012 by

Caroline Brannigan
Richmond, North Yorkshire

www.carolinebrannigan.com
01748 821041

ISBN: 978-0-9568700-7-0

Printed in the UK by the MPG Biddles Group
Bodmin and King's Lynn

This book is dedicated to all my relatives who have made me feel so at home in a distant land and to the staff at Bristol Records Office and Downend Library, South Gloucestershire

Prologue

The book "There's One Born Every Minute" is about my life, 90 years in 90 pages. I could have expanded it, as I later found out, but as I am used to writing reports of events I tend to leave out the less relevant parts and so it was with my life history.

In this the sequel, I will try to rectify the omission but at the same time try not to be boring.

Sunny Jim was born in 1903 and soon became a nationally known character advertising "Force", the first ready to eat breakfast cereal manufactured by Nestlé. The advert quotes:

"High o'er the fence leaps Sunny Jim; Force is the food that raises him."

I am sure many people have been nicknamed "Sunny Jim". I am not the first nor will I be the last. It has stuck with me for 90 years and I prefer it to my birth name.

Writing is an art. It has been with us since mankind wrote with sticks in mud and sand and has progressed through various forms until Mr Biro came along and designed an instrument which could be operated under adverse conditions.

Initially, writing was done pictorially in the eastern continents and if one looks at Chinese and similar characters this is still the basis of their writing mode. Theirs is done pictorially whilst the western world is done phonetically. The art of writing is dying because of the modern system of communication. No longer do we have a person with a message in a split stick, covering miles on foot. All one now has to do is press a few keys and the message is transferred over miles.

This was proved to me when my manuscript for "There's One Born Every Minute" moved some 200 miles in a few minutes.

My foster mother used to write every day to one or two of her many relatives and when I was struggling with school essays I asked, "How can you write so much?" The reply was, "Write whatever comes into your head relative to the matter on which you are thinking, some other person may be interested."

And so today, following mother's comments, I can write about most things after some research.

When I started writing "There's One Born Every Minute" I had occasion to look at a number of documents hidden amongst many others in the Family Bible. This gave me the idea to write what I could of the several families noted from this research and also to further delve into my birth family records of which I knew very little. It is surprising what one uncovers.

Chapter One

Bristol was a great seafaring port and as such needed men who had trades to keep ships "shipshape and Bristol fashion". James Gardiner who was born in the early 19ᵗʰ century (around 1840) was a shipwright, a very skilled job which commanded respect.

I have no record of whom he married or when, but together they produced four children, three girls and a boy - Caroline, Matilda and another girl whose name I am unable to recall, together with Thomas.

Because James was a skilled tradesman and was as a consequence earning good money, he was able to send his children to school. Payment for school lessons is not a new thing and whilst the payment required was not great, it was more than many could afford. Food came first.

Thomas was born in 1867, he left school when about 12 years of age and went to work in a hotel kitchen as general "dogsbody". In this manner he learnt the rudiments of kitchen life and gradually climbed the ladder, learning to be a chef. It was very hard and tiring work and long hours (he never went to bed before midnight and he had to be up and working by 5am for breakfast) but through perseverance, he saved enough money to join forces with another similarly minded person (a German) and together they bought a hotel in Belfast. This was all before the First World War and here Thomas met a girl whom he courted and married. However, the marriage did not last very long as the woman died in childbirth. All her pregnancies ended in stillborn births and I can only surmise that in the last birth with the child dead, the poison spread to the mother and caused a fever.

After some discussion with his partner, they decided to sell up and go their separate ways, the one to Germany and Thomas to England and his home city of Bristol. The year was about 1907 and from the sale of the property in Ireland (half of which went to the partner) Thomas bought property in Horfield. In those days, houses were "two a penny" but it was not a good deal as the rents did not meet the repair bills (Mr Micawber strikes again).

Immediately after arriving in Bristol from Ireland, Thomas needed somewhere to live so he persuaded his youngest sister to allow him a room in their house in Clifton. She had married another chef by the name of Edwin Harvey (a well-known Bristol name).

For a while we will leave this section of the web and transfer to Bath.

Chapter Two

As the name implies, a wheeler is a person who is involved in the art of building wheels (a wheelwright). Although Daniel Wheeler was a cabinet maker, I presume his father, Henry, was also involved in the wood trade and so Daniel carried on the family tradition. In the early 19th century, the son usually followed the father in his trade and in fact became an apprentice of the father.

I know nothing of Daniel's life, but he married Louise Simmonds in 1866. They had both been born in 1840. Between them they had four children, three girls and a boy, Emily Kate (1866), Mary Sarah (1868), Daniel (1869) and Louisa (1871). Mary Sarah was in later life to become my foster mother.

Times were hard and whilst Daniel (father) was a cabinet maker, the trade was not very well paid. Regrettably he died in 1872 aged 31 years so his wife, being a milliner, turned her hand to her trade, making hats to raise the house income. In those days few people, if any, went outside without wearing some head covering. This also occurred indoors, maybe because of ill-fitting doors and windows.

At this time at 15 Northampton Street, Bath, there was a brewery cum public house named The White Horse, owned by a Mr Edwin Harvey who was by marriage a relation (brother-in-law) to Louisa Wheeler, the mother of the four children.

When he and his wife saw the state of the finances in the Wheeler household, both of them offered to foster Mary Sarah who, unbeknown to her, was to become unpaid general factotum, looking after a not well woman, working in the business, cooking, cleaning, serving meals and liquor from dawn 'til dusk. It was work from 5.30am to 11pm throughout the week.

Mary Sarah's brother Daniel did no better as he worked similar hours in a hotel in the city for a pittance but they did have a flat supplied. The other two sisters fared a little better, the one more than the other. Emily Kate married the son of a well-known grocer (J. Honeybone). They lived in the Widcombe area of Bath, in a stone fronted property. They had one girl child but I know little of them as I recall my foster mother only took me to see them on one occasion. Unlike the younger sister's approach, I had to sit in a chair and not move until it was time to leave – it certainly was a very strict household.

This younger sister Louisa married a council employee who was a ganger foreman in the Highway Division of Bath City Council (James Francis).

They produced eighteen children and adopted one, which I believe was the product of a union of the oldest daughter with some unknown man.

Louisa tried to persuade Mary Sarah to adopt James Francis (the offspring of the eldest daughter) but Mary Sarah's husband would have none of it and for some long time afterward the two sisters did not see eye to eye.

Chapter Three

You will remember in the first chapter, the name "Edwin Harvey" cropped up as being the husband of Matilda (née Gardiner). He happened to be the nephew of one Edwin Harvey, proprietor of The White Horse public house and brewery in Northampton Street, Bath, who was also the uncle of Mary Sarah Wheeler.

One hundred years ago, marriages were arranged and

you will also recall in chapter one that as a temporary measure, Thomas Gardiner was staying with his sister and brother-in-law.

Feeling that her brother needed female company, she asked her husband to invite his cousin to tea in the hope that a friendship would generate. The invitation was accepted and on arrival in Bristol, Mary Sarah was taken to the house in Clifton where purely by chance (or so it seemed) Thomas happened to be in the house and so was introduced. Both these people were very handsome and so, after tea, Thomas asked if Mary Sarah would like to walk to Clifton Downs. These walks continued after each visit until they came to an understanding.

After a short courtship, they married at St Peter's Church, Clifton Wood, on 21st October 1908, Mary Sarah aged 40 and Thomas aged 41. No longer was there any room in the Clifton house for two families so they moved to one of the many properties Thomas owned in Horfield, where they lived for some 12 years. During this period, Mary Sarah had several miscarriages which upset both of them. They then presumed they would have no offspring to raise, but this would change.

Chapter Four

The base of Family Cullimore is on the eastern banks of the Severn Estuary ranging between Bristol and Gloucester. In the transept of St Mary the Virgin, Thornbury is a slate tomb plaque situated to the north side of the church bearing an inscription from 1807 to Martha Cullimore Died September 6th Age 67 years. The inscription reads,

Stay gentle reader, haste thou not away
Cast back thine eyes on me poor lump of clay
For thou, like me, lye down in silence must
Enclosed within a gloomy bed of dust
Till the last day when God us both shall raise
With saints to sing and celebrate his praise
And seat us on a throne void of all harmes
Evermore to crown us with immortal charmes

As a consequence of the above, I falsely assumed my branch of the family Cullimore came from the Thornbury area and so I searched churchyards in that general area hoping to find deceased relatives but I was searching in the wrong area.

Earlier I said we were a prolific family ranging between Bristol and Gloucester on the banks of the Severn Estuary and some 10 miles inland. It wasn't until I got my library staff interested in my search that I found my branch lived not in the Thornbury and Gloucester area but in Hallen and Crooks Marsh which was then in the county of Gloucestershire.

My grandparents farmed at two farms on the low lying land at Hallen, "Madams Farm" and "Pack Gate Farm", very poor, waterlogged ground as I found on a recent visit. The farms are long gone and the land is now under a motorway. The Avonmouth Development Corporation took over a great deal of the farms of grandparents and great grandparents. They owned Crooks Marsh Farm and an adjacent property.

George Leonard Cullimore (grandfather) married Mary Anne Petherham (grandmother) of Crooks Marsh Farm and they raised two children, a boy, George Leonard Cullimore and a girl, Mary Leonard Cullimore (birth mother to myself and my sister). Mary grew up and gave birth to a child out of wedlock in 1920, which turned out to be me. The small boy child was born in Southmead Infirmary, three months premature. It was felt that the child's mother would be unable to successfully raise this infant, covered in eczema as he was, with no nails, bald as a coot and with eyes still closed.

They didn't have equipment in those days as they do today. It was either live or die. An advert was placed in the Births, Marriages and Deaths section of the local paper, "Baby needing a loving new home".

By good fortune (for the baby), Mary Sarah Gardiner noticed the advert and drew the attention of her husband to it. Knowing how much his wife missed having such an item (remember the consideration given to James Francis) he arranged a visit by the mother and grandmother and after many questions decided on a transfer.

Beyond an abbreviated birth certificate, no paperwork changed hands and there were no official adoption papers, the child was just handed over as a parcel. The subsequent problems experienced by that small morsel (2½ lb) was a lesson learnt the hard way.

Eight years later a girl child was born of that same lady who had borne the 2½ lb boy child, this time through a bigamous marriage by the man.

Chapter Five

Thomas and Mary Sarah Gardiner were now in their 60s and living in the country in a now grade II listed farmhouse to which they had moved when they took charge of that very small 2½ lb morsel. He was now eight years of age and, suffering tonsillitis, had to go to Berkeley Hospital to have his tonsils removed. On being discharged from the hospital on the following day and delivered home with a very sore throat, he found a tea party in full swing.

Around a very large kitchen table sat Thomas and Mary Sarah, their lady lodger and two strangers, one of whom was nursing a small child. I was introduced in the manner "This is your Aunt Mary and this is Sissy", nothing mentioned about the baby.

Both these persons tried to engage me with the baby but, being shy, I was having none of it. I was much later to learn that these people were my natural grandmother and my natural mother and my half-sister whom they had brought in the hope she would be accepted into the "Gardiner" family and bond with myself, as a joint family.

It was bad enough to bring up one small, weak child when one was 50 years old and with all the problems that incurs. The small morsel in the arms of her mother was whole and hearty but it was felt by my foster parents that it would be too much of a responsibility for people of their age to take on. After retiring to another room to discuss the matter, Thomas and Mary Sarah returned to advise they could not take on any extra burden, so the baby should remain with her mother.

In subsequent years, after I found out that the little baby was my half sister, it was regretted by me that we were brought up as cousins in different households. I had to call my natural grandmother "Aunt Mary". I never addressed my natural mother as anything and only saw her twice in all of my life.

The little baby girl was called Norah. As we grew up, both she and our grandmother spent many holidays with us, to get some bonding factor going I suppose. So in spite of us living with different families over the years, a bond did exist.

Our grandmother was a strict disciplinarian and I well remember my sister, aged about four, needing to go to the toilet. In those days there was no modern flush system and we had a closet in a brick shed at the bottom of the garden shielded by a plum tree and a hazelnut tree. I was instructed to take my sister (as I now know her) to this toilet and because she was so young, I had to lift her on to the seat, arrange for her undergarment to be removed and hold her in position so she would not fall through the large hole in the seat.

I remember it as if it were only yesterday, our grandmother walking up the garden path with my foster mother and noticing we were both in the toilet together and being harangued for being in that situation.

We of course thought nothing of it at the time and it was only many years later did I ever consider the issue to be of a sexual nature, after all we were only about four and 11 years old and such things did not occur in young heads in those days.

At 11 years of age, I was off to Grammar School for some five years. I was not very academic as proven by my school reports and every quarter my father would read, "Could do better if only he would try". My head was always somewhere else and the only subjects which attracted me were art, English, botany and geography. The French master and I disagreed on my first day and this lasted for five years.

On the first day one had to be indoctrinated which meant going through a ritual. One could either accept the situation or say No. The No brigade were few and far between as this meant one was ostracised for the whole of one's stay.

The immersion of head in water was no problem as I could stay under water for three minutes but the second test of putting your finger into a 240-volt light socket was a bit drastic. The inducers never considered that death might occur and the only recall I have is of finding myself in the cloakroom corner on the floor, with the words "you have passed". I certainly had. I had passed out.

Chapter Six

On leaving school at 16 years of age I had to find a job and whilst I suggested farming (my grandparents and great grandparents were all farmers), neither grandmother or my foster father would have me go into a 24/7 business. When I mentioned following Thomas into the hotel business he said I was not strong enough to stand such a hectic 18/7 as he had done.

I was adept at mechanical things, due I feel to my Meccano which I had as a Christmas present some 10 years before, so after looking around, it was decided to apprentice me with a large engineering firm some six miles away in the next town.

My father Thomas (he has been that to me ever since I was fostered) took me to see the personnel manager, but prior to my interview, both father and the manager (Sam Marshall) went off to talk.

I always wondered why, when entering school, work or some similar establishment where my birth certificate had to be produced this was done in a surreptitious manner (but more of that later).

I got the placement and spent six months at the training school under a very good tutor who was coming up for retirement. Little did I know at the time, but he was the uncle of the girl I should meet in a short time.

Our training school was adjacent to the works offices and in my book "There's One Born Every Minute" I described how I noticed a girl looking from a window at the various workmen passing by. Who noticed whom first, I have no idea, but the shape of the face and the Romanesque nose took my fancy. After much chasing (on my part) and by some suggestion by her mother (when asked for advice), we eventually got together in a walking out part, me 17 years of age and the girl 15. At lunchtimes I would walk her part of the way home to lunch and then wait until she returned.

I dared not tell my father of this as he would have put a stop to it at once but, as it happened, he had no chance to do so. He had waterworks problems and after much discussion with our doctor and a fellow who had recently had a similar operation, he decided on action and went into Bristol Infirmary.

Unlike today and the modern improvements, it took two operations over three weeks and, regrettably, after internal bleeding after the second operation, father died. I sat at his bedside for long periods but to no avail and I had to leave all the subsequent arrangements to his nephew who was older than me by some four years.

After the return home and the funeral, there followed months of worry, not only for Mary Sarah but also for me having to manage things I knew nothing about nor did Mary Sarah, as Thomas had handled all financial matters.

Thomas Gardiner (1867 – 1938) died intestate. He was very good at handling all his sister's business but not his own. All his money went to the State except for £1,000 to Mary Sarah from which she had to purchase the estate, leaving very little in hand.

All she now had was a 10-shilling widow's pension and an annuity of 10 shillings per month from her uncle's estate in Bath. There was no way for us to get by on such meagre finances, seeing how large the property was. The matter was left for a while for some decision to be made as how to overcome this problem (Mr Micawber hovering in the wings).

Adding problem to problem, I said to Mother, "I am courting a girl at work" and with the words ringing in my ears "Bring her to Sunday tea" I also heard her add, "I have something to show you".

Of course I wondered what that might be and within the space of a few minutes two documents were produced, the one my baptismal certificate bearing one name, the second an abbreviated birth certificate showing another. Now I knew why father always went with me on official business and why, in some instances, I was treated in a strange manner. Mother apologised and said, "We should have told you long ago but were always afraid so to do."

Now I had three names, which should I use? My known name of plain Gardiner, my baptismal name of Cullimore-Gardiner or that on this brief birth certificate, Wride-Cullimore.

I had been using the name of my foster parents for 18 years and I supposed I should go on doing so but things changed. I told my girl and her parents, who were all very understanding, and my girl said, "It doesn't matter what your name is, you are you."

Chapter Seven

Now I need to say a little about my wife's family. She was Barbara Annie Bloodworth and was born in 1922. Sadly, she died in 2009. We had been married for nearly 70 years. Some of her ancestors were Morland, which was a well known name in the Stroud Valley and they had a factory at Gloucester making matches (England's Glory). Regrettably, one of the family was a bit of a spendthrift, became penniless and asked for a hand out.

This was offered with the proviso that he changed his surname. After some thought, the name Marling came to mind, which he adopted. This should not mean however "the sins of the fathers should descend on the children."

They have to live their own lives. Further down the line, my wife's grandfather, William Henry Marling, a young, fit and strong person, worked as a boiler maker with the railway. He somehow got to meet a young girl, Rosa Annie Harvey, from the village of Nympsfield on top of the Cotswolds.

Producing children is done the same way the world over and testing sometimes means more than the word implies. Youngsters will do it and in this instance Rosa Annie fell pregnant. She worked as a lady's maid in a large house and to save trouble William and Rosa ran away to Doncaster to get married and to carry on with William's job as a boiler maker in the railway works. A daughter was born and named Rosa after her mother. This Rosa was my wife's mother. Here the family remained for some period when the second girl child, Elsie, was born in 1907.

In 1914 the whole family return to the hamlet of Nupend on the Cotswolds from where William got a job in the valley at an engineering works. To save the long walk to and from work, he found a terraced cottage in the village of Cam. Very close to his employment, the cottage was a two up, two down, scullery in an outhouse common to all the rank and a toilet at the bottom of the garden (a three seater).

Rosa Annie had enough to do, keeping two girls under her thumb and although the older girl was always quiet and thoughtful, her sister Elsie was always self-centred and so it continued throughout their lives.

Chapter Eight

Fast forward to the start of the Second World War. Elsie was a live wire in the village and she, with her friends, played tennis and golf, went dancing and spent all her earnings on number one so it is not surprising that when all the other girls had boyfriends she was not going to be left out.

How she met her first boyfriend, I have no idea. Samuel Gabb came from a mining town in South Wales. Miners suffered terrible lung complaints so when he was diagnosed as having TB this was a sad blow and it wasn't long after the diagnosis that he died and perhaps what followed was on the rebound. Reginald Gabb, the brother of Samuel, saw an opportunity not to be missed and started paying attention to this dashing young lady. It wasn't long before they were married and, after a short honeymoon, he was called up. He was a sailor and a torpedo man in the Royal Navy detailed to join the aircraft carrier "Glorious" which was to operate in the North Sea in the Finland/Norway area.

Norway was being invaded and British troops were sent to help defend that country. Regrettably, the British were not accustomed to fighting in the conditions presented to them, the German opposition too strong, the British ill equipped. Things looked bad for the Norwegian Royal Family and a group of ships were sent to bring King Hakon and his family to England. The Glorious was one of those ships and it has always been assumed she was to act as a decoy for the destroyer carrying the royal family. As things turned out, the British forces had to retreat. Many were left dead or as prisoners. The Glorious was identified by the battleship "Graf Spey" which, with her massive armament, sunk the aircraft carrier. Only six personnel survived in one lifeboat, some 1,400 complement went to an icy death. In all the books I have read about the Second World War, no mention has ever been noted of this particular encounter.

Elsie Gabb was now pregnant, a war widow and hating every minute of it. Gone were the days that her friends were still enjoying. She went back to work for a period until her situation prevented further work, then she was banished to her older sister's bungalow which had been built in the rickyard of the father of her brother-in-law.

A boy child was born and after a short period of recuperation, the mother returned to work, leaving the care of the baby to the grandmother. Money being so tight in those days, every chance of earning had to be taken.

Chapter Nine

In the previous chapter I mentioned that Elsie Gabb went to a bungalow to have her child. The building of this bungalow was occasioned by the fact that the local doctor recommended that Barbara Annie Bloodworth, the daughter of the older sister, be moved from the valley of the River Cam where the air was damp and oppressive to a cleaner air quality.

A discussion took place between William Joseph Bloodworth (owner of a farm at Uleyfields) and William Reginald Bloodworth (son) and father of Barbara. Agreement was reached that the new property could be built in the rickyard of the farm. After a trip to the local building society, sufficient funds were released to build. This was about 1929 when wages for a skilled man were a guinea a week, with a total debt of £450 on the bungalow and a 25 year mortgage at something like 10s 6d (currently 53p), food, heating and all other matters attendant to house owning, it was going to be an uphill struggle.

Nevertheless, by both parents working hard, going out rabbiting, picking berries from the hedgerows and collecting fallen wood for the fire, they survived. The daughter grew in strength simply by walking to school over hilly ground, some mile and a half and then back again at tea time.

The school was a typical village school, no academia just the 3 Rs and knitting, sewing and cooking, all in preparation for life as a housewife. Strangely enough, the first words I said to my future mother-in-law were "Can she cook?"

Age 14, Barbara was sent off to work in the cost office of the same engineering works as her maternal grandfather, her father and myself which is how we all eventually met.

Chapter Ten

The Bloodworths have a large and extended family (much like our own). The joke has been that should one call the name "Bloodworth" in the town of Dursley, most people would think they were being addressed.

William Joseph Bloodworth was a farmer at Uleyfields, a hamlet about 1½ miles east of Dursley, a Cotswold market town, and Uley, noted for its prehistoric barrow.

He married a cousin, Annie (née Bloodworth) and together they produced three sons and two daughters. The strain of bearing five children and doing the various farm chores made Annie ill and as a consequence when the children were old enough, they had to knuckle down and do housework for the girls and farm work for the boys.

Their father, having a large milk round, had to start early in the morning, milk the cows, harness the horse to the milk cart, load the churns and complete his round all before breakfast time of a normal household. More often than not, the horse would stop at the farm gate and the driver would then wake up, dismount and go in the kitchen for his breakfast which the girls would have prepared after cleaning the house prior to going to school. The boys had also to do their share by unhitching the horse from the trap, giving it a feed and water and brushing it down, then put it to grass before going off to school. I can see why I was dissuaded from farming.

When the eldest son, Albert, became of age, his father sold him the farm and he (the father) from said proceeds had a house built some half a mile away. The milk round was sold to the youngest son, Alan, which left the middle son to work at the engineering firm.

William Reginald Bloodworth was that middle son and I presume whilst helping his father on the milk round at a weekend met a girl some two miles away. That girl Rosa Annie Marling (born 1900 died 1980) turned out to be the finest mother-in-law one could ever wish to have.

William Reginald and Rosa Annie were married in 1921 and produced a girl child in 1922 who they named Barbara Annie (the girl I chased after for five years). The doctor who attended the birth was ham fisted and as a consequence of his actions, Rosa Annie was never to conceive again, in fact she was so damaged that she rejected all advances by her husband. The baby was extracted by forceps so viciously that the baby's ribs were crushed and as a result she suffered deformity all her life. The parents doted on her, especially her father who, because he was interested in sport (although never taking any active part in any such activity), took his daughter to watch most things. They both got up early to listen to cricket or boxing on the radio if that was taking place in another part of the world.

I don't know whether my foster mother Mary Sarah had second sight but after I had taken Barbara to Sunday tea with her, I was asked to look for someone else. No explanation was given but I read between the lines. I was besotted with this girl and I was not going to let her go on what I presumed was a whim of mothers. My visits to her home at

Uleyfields increased and I always tell people we that treated each other as brother and sister, one never seen without the other.

After courting for some three years, I asked Barbara's father if we could marry and move to a property I had my eye on for £450. His answer was of course, "Not yet, you are still young and not up to the rigours of marriage and a house." Of course he was perfectly correct about this, he had been through the same moves.

Chapter 11

In 1939 Barbara and I got engaged. I was earning a basic engineering wage of seven shillings and sixpence per week. I gave mother five shillings, the balance was for possible bus fares to work should the weather be inclement. From this balance of two shillings and sixpence I saved enough to buy a diamond ring, no way worth a great deal but all I could afford. It was a token of my esteem and that is all I can say about it.

I was 19 and Barbara was 17, we went everywhere together, liked the same things, had the same political ideals, so we were a couple.

It was coming up to Christmas and my mother suggested that Barbara and her family come to our house for that period. It snowed heavily and since the bus had to negotiate three very steep hills, they were withdrawn. Not to disappoint my mother, it was decided we would walk the seven miles that separated us. It was struggle with many stops on the way but we arrived exhausted and thankful for the large fire roaring in the grate.

My future parents-in-law were surprised at the large house we lived in and the amount of attached land. They were under the impression they were only coming to tea but because of the state of the weather they stayed overnight after mother had made up a bed for the three of them. The buses returned to service, the snow having dissipated, and everyone went their various ways – Bloodworths to Uleyfields and mother and I remained at home to discuss what to do for the future.

The current property was far too large and expensive to run on our income and mother felt she would be better off moving back to Bristol. Things were set in motion, the house was up for sale and bought for peanuts and from this money a house was bought in Bishopston, Bristol. We moved in but immediately I disliked the property, giving no consideration to the reason for the move.

Because of the distance between our new premises and my work I had to give in my notice. The personnel manager was very understanding of the situation, he wished me good luck and said that if I should ever have occasion to want to return, there was a job waiting. This showed they did consider their employees' welfare.

The first job I went for in the new area, I got. I went for a medical and was classed as "C3 feet". I still have them today, in a terrible condition (pride comes before a fall). Always buy shoes for comfort, never for show. Deformed feet are made by bad cobblers.

Because of my dermatitis caused by using caustic in my previous employment, I was given a job in the Research Department where I could operate on materials which needed no cooling fluid.

A group of us produced items evolved in the mind of our manager and the War Department in an attempt to combat those ideas produced by the enemy. The trouble was that not only were we trying to beat the enemy but also our own side as several other firms were trying to produce identical items. I have only found out about this in recent years by reading books on innovations made during the Second World War.

We had all been sworn to secrecy and had signed documents to that effect (I have signed similar documents three times). I was now earning the vast sum of 25 shillings per week which I now felt was sufficient for two people to live on, so on my next visit to see Barbara I again put the question of marriage to her father. An answer was not immediate so Barbara approached her mother to pressure her father with a parting shot that if the answer was in the negative she would move in with me. This very defiant statement showed she was in earnest and so permission was granted.

For three years we had been travelling the 25 miles house to house, Barbara every fortnight and me whenever circumstances permitted. I was working day and night shift, doing fire watching and on call for ARP rescue duty 6pm – 6am.

The wedding was scheduled for 21st November 1942 when Barbara was 20 and I was 22. We asked my mother if she would attend but she regretfully declined (she still disagreed with the union). I learn today that I also invited my natural grandmother but I cannot remember so doing.

We married at the Methodist Church in Dursley where Barbara's parents were married. Only a few people attended - Barbara's parents, her maternal grandparents, her Aunt

Elsie with son Richard George Gabb (my Godson) and an elderly lady from an adjacent hamlet who had known Barbara all her life. Of course, I must not forget the Best Man who had been lodging with my mother whilst drafted from Fowey in Cornwall to a training establishment in Bristol.

The ceremony over, we all went to the Marling cottage for our wedding breakfast, which, because food was on coupons, had been won by fair means and foul.

I well remember the first time I had visited the property. I was invited (commanded) to tea so that Granny could see how I addressed the table (as a young girl she had been in service in a large house on top of the Cotswolds so knew the ropes). Fortunately I had been taught from a very young age how to do that very thing. Granny wasn't going to allow her granddaughter to attach herself to any "hobble-de-hoy".

The afternoon saw us and the best man go to the local railway station and head for our Bristol address. My foster mother Mary Sarah had arranged to visit her youngest sister Louisa in Bath for the weekend, the best man had found alternative accommodation and we were left on our own to enjoy our own company.

On the Monday morning, we both took a walk of about ½ mile to a local photographer's premises to have a record of what we looked like on our wedding day, my dear wife in her fur coat which I had purchased as a wedding present and me in my chalk striped grey suit.

We returned to our Bishopston address to cook lunch and then in the afternoon I saw Barbara on to a bus for her trip home and for the next six months we saw each other whenever circumstances allowed.

As I have previously expressed, Mary Sarah and Barbara

never saw eye to eye so in the next six months I set about flat hunting. I found one in Clifton at a price we could afford and pointed the matter out to mother who understood the situation so she decided to do the same but move nearer to her direct relatives in Bath. She found two rooms in a house in The Abbey Church Yard and we moved her furniture (which wasn't a great deal) and she settled in. This gave me some time to deal with our own accommodation and the next time Barbara came to Bristol I met her at the bus station and took her to see this flat I had found.

There were 72 stairs up to four rooms. Barbara's face fell, she turned to me and said, "We can't live here". It certainly needed cleaning and on reporting back to base, her mother and father came down the following Friday and with elbow grease transformed the flat for which I was very grateful.

After these preparations, we both moved in with some of mother's furniture which she had no room for in her two rooms. Two homemade beds and a cat, well, really a kitten we had accepted from the people in the ground floor flat. Not only was it riddled with fleas, it also fell through four panes of glass covering the well of the property (not a water well I might add), the skylight which allowed such light to the well of the stairs. It cost me a lot of money to repair the glass and to stop it happening again. I covered the access with chicken wire.

I de-flead the cat, provided it with a litter box and it drove all the many mice into other people's flats. Barbara would buy it best cod every day from McFisheries in Baldwin Street. This was a ritual, she didn't have to say anything on going in, she was just handed the packet of fish, paid at the counter and came home. Spike, as the cat was called, would sit on the stove whilst the fish cooked with its head covered in steam, waiting for the feast. Barbara would always have tea ready when I arrived at the front door because the cat was so used to the sound of my motorcycle it would run to the window looking for me to turn into the driveway.

We only intended to stay in the flat for six months, we left fifteen years later when an endowment policy I had been paying into (since I was in my late teens) fell due and we were then able to put a deposit on a cottage some eight miles away on the other side of town in the suburb of Downend.

Had my father-in-law agreed to go guarantor on the house I originally had my eye on, it would have saved us £1,300 but he was afraid the property would be bombed and we should all be the poorer. As it is, that property still stands at a value far in excess of its original £450.

Prior to our marriage we had discussions with the minister regarding the dual names I bore. After a long thought, he said "I will use both names in the ceremony and on the marriage certificate so we know you are officially married." To my mind, my wife was the only person to be married to a dual named person.

Chapter 12

Bricks and mortar always cost a lot of money, the longer one leaves the purchase, the dearer it becomes (the pound devalues quickly). After the very bad winter of 1947 when we had snow for weeks on end and freezing temperatures, all the pipes were frozen and we had to walk to the toilets next the suspension bridge to deal with our own needs. The thaw set in, the roof of our block of flats was not felted and the snow had blown under the tiles to lie thick on the rafters as, I assumed, there was no way into the roof void for any inspection. For four weeks the melted snow ran down the inside wall of our flat, through the floor and down to the ground floor (we were the top flat of five).

I was offered the property for £1,750 but now knowing the state of the roof I declined but said, "You repair the roof and I will buy". Needless to say this offer was rejected as the cost of felting and retiling and the scaffolding needed to do the job would have been very expensive.

About 1964 we noticed a cottage for sale at the same price of £1,750, my endowment was now due and so off I went to the bank manager for a loan of £1,000 over a 25 year repayment period. All was agreed and we bought two adjoining cottages, one for us, the other was occupied. When this matter came before the local council, the occupied cottage was declared unfit and the tenant removed to sheltered accommodation. We were going to work on it to bring it up to standard but our finances did not allow this so it was set aside as a store and workshop.

By this time my wife's parents had retired and they wanted to be closer to their daughter. We discussed this at great length and it was eventually decided both families should live in the one house, my parents-in-law on the ground floor and we on the first with a shared kitchen.

In this instance, the two women were of the same family so there was little animosity. In any case, we were not at home so very often that we got into each other's way. We were involved in motor sport, both during the week and always at weekends so this left the house mainly to Barbara's parents and the cat. In the evenings I would be in the workshop building trailers and Barbara would be doing secretarial work.

This system carried on for several years until my father-in-law suffered from what is now classified as Parkinson's Disease and mother from a "dicky" heart condition. As both of us were at work, the doctor suggested they be transferred to social care and a place was found for them at a residential home locally.

Once again we had a visiting job to do which we did each evening. Initially they were separated but they so pined for each other that they were given a double room and looked after by a very good staff. Regrettably they both suffered deterioration in their general being and had to be hospitalised where they eventually succumbed.

This left us on our own for really the first time for a long period, but we weren't able to use the time to much advantage as now the cat had to be looked after by ourselves. Barbara was also finding it difficult climbing the stairs and in general conversation we let it be known we were looking for a bungalow.

By a quirk of fate a long standing friend (a nephew of Mary Sarah's) heard that a neighbour of his was selling up and would we like to view the property. Leaving Barbara at home I jumped into his car to inspect the premises and on being introduced to the sellers, walked around both the bungalow and garden, decided then and there this was what we were looking for and I said to the couple, "I'll buy it" not asking the price.

The year was 1979 and visiting the bank manager yet

again, I put the case to him for another loan over a 15 year period to which he agreed. I expected to sell our cottage quickly. The workshop I sold to my next-door neighbour so he could extend his property for his growing family, our cottage was sold to a builder who was intending to do improvements by knocking down a supporting wall which, although I warned what would happen, proved the point after the roof fell in. He vowed he would take me to court over this matter but, having signed the contract, this action never took place and he had to do a complete rebuild.

Part of the garden was sold to yet another neighbour for him to erect a garage. A JCB was brought in to move the soil mound and an old plum tree. In doing this operation the JCB bucket hit a large stone and, on further work, this stone was dislodged to fall into a void with a splash.

When we bought the cottages I was advised by the next-door neighbour there was a well underneath and that the overflow evacuated through a grill in our garden wall across a cobbled way in the main road and on past the Manor House. The advice I was given I put aside only now to be proved correct as on putting a long ladder through the hole made by dislodging the capping stone it was found to be a large stone tank for the Manor House and the many cottages which it supported. The water supply came from a spring which rose in the local park, and still does, it carries on as an open stream past my current property and on as a leat to the River Frome at Hambrook.

This water catchment site is now recorded in the annals of Kingswood Borough Council who had the void capped as a source of water should we suffer some atomic disaster.

The bungalow cost us ten times that of the cottages some 15 years before and I took out a mortgage over a 15 year period. Being at the time in a well-paid job (24/7), I took the bull by the horns and paid off twice the required sum every month and so discharged the debt in eight years.

Fast traffic passed our frontage and animals suffered as a consequence. Our cats were not immune to being knocked over by this traffic and after two had been killed in this manner we resigned ourselves to being without such interesting animals. I have had cats most of my life, they are independent beings and only need feeding, warmth and shelter.

Our interest was in auto sport at which we had a good innings but then it moved on to politics and took up all our time to do it justice. Not only was I on the District Council but both Barbara and I were on the Parish Council as well.

Her family suffered from a hereditary condition of glaucoma, an eye problem which is a progressive disease causing blindness. On examination she was asked if she would be a guinea pig for a new treatment devised at the Bristol Eye Hospital and overseen by a doctor from South Africa. She agreed and for 15 years attended for said treatment until she was asked to present herself for an operation which initially went very well but subsequently she deteriorated and was left blind. As a consequence, I gave up politics at the Unitary Authority stage to devote my time to looking after my dear wife.

I have had a good innings politically, having reached the stage of Mayor of a Borough and Chairman of my Unitary Authority and still represent my Parish Ward, for one year becoming Chairman.

Chapter 13

Baby Richard George Gabb, Elsie's son, Barbara's cousin and my Godson, was growing up fast and every now and then he came to Bristol to give his granny a rest. When he was about four years of age, Barbara was not working at the time, (this was during the war years and the Ministry of Employment hadn't yet caught up with her). She took him to many places of interest, not only for his sake but to also learn something herself.

The one thing that sticks in his mind is being walked across the Clifton Suspension Bridge, dropping a small piece of gravel through a crack in the walkway then saying he saw it splash in the water. That was 70 years ago and he still brings it forward in his mind. The brain works in a peculiar way; it is how I am writing this epistle.

He was very close to his cousin and we took him to different places to broaden his mind. He came to an age when he had to attend preparatory school and although we had done our best, he lacked confidence. I felt this had been brought on by his mother. However, he was allocated to my old school some six miles from home as a boarder until nine years of age when he then transferred to a school nearer his home.

He was not strong, suffered a lot with chest complaints (hereditary, and still does at 70-plus) so ill health impeded his scholarly progress. However when it was time to leave and search for work, those in the know got him a job at the local cloth factory where his mother worked.

He was trained as a time and motion person and learned the trade. Having served his apprenticeship, he moved on and got a job in Cheltenham at the newly formed business of British Nylon Spinners. He had to travel there daily so I got him an A30 Austin car and taught him to drive and saw that he passed his test. He was now on his own two feet.

Having to visit the post office near where he worked in Cheltenham, he struck up a friendship with a girl. He discovered there was a long-standing feud going on between her family and his and Elsie Gabb was totally against her son having anything to do with this girl.

Nevertheless, they got engaged and on the Saturday morning of the wedding we were all in the church waiting. The vicar asked for the registrar's certificate, only to find there had been a mix-up. The registrar had gone on holiday and his assistant, who was some 15 miles away, knew nothing of any proposed wedding.

We were all requested to calmly wait until someone collected the paperwork. The bride-to-be sat in the vestry with her entourage and Richard George was being pressed by his mother to defect from the impending marriage as she saw this hiatus as an omen.

After waiting for some two hours (fortunately it was not raining), the whole matter was resolved and I have always said, "Thank God he married a down-to-earth woman". Over the years she has been the stabilising partner. They produced two children, a girl and then some two years later, a boy.

Chapter 14

I have said that after our marriage mother moved to Bath, but by this time she was not as fit as I would like her to have been, though she managed the small apartment well enough. It was not very costly to run.

I visited her during the week and Barbara and I both went at weekends and I asked a certain niece of hers to call in on occasions and to telephone me should anything be untoward.

Mother had been in her younger days a very strong woman. One day the niece telephoned to say mother had had a stroke but was at present still in the apartment. I dropped everything to rush to see her. She was in a very bad state and I called upon the doctor with whom she was registered to ask his advice. He said that under the circumstances, it would be best that she transfer to St Martin's Hospital where she would be under constant care by the nursing staff.

This was quickly arranged and the prompt action was a blessing, she could not have a better place in which she could have attention night and day. Both speech and her right arm were affected.

This all happened in 1949, I was 29 and I asked mother if I could have permission to buy a motorcycle to ease the drain on my pocket in visiting every other day from some

15 miles away by train and bus. With the words ringing in my ears, "You know what your father would say" she eventually agreed and I spent the vast sum of £27 on a piece of transport.

I had to rebuild it to do the journey and I also had to pass my driving test. On the first test, the machine broke down. I was then offered a free retest which I took the following week and passed with "flying colours". This then was my transport to and from work every day and to Bath during the week.

At weekends Barbara and I would travel by bus to sit with mother for some period. She could not move her arm and could only mumble but did manage to convey some information to us. This situation carried on for about two years, when, after the fifth stroke she succumbed.

It was then my sad duty to arrange burial in the family grave along with father who had died in 1938 age 72. Mother died in 1951 aged 83.

Chapter 15

The purchase of a motorcycle was the start of an interest for both of us. I had been interested in mechanical things from a very early age so it came as no surprise to seek to join a motorcycle club.

We considered going to a club meeting held every Tuesday at 7pm in The Full Moon public house in Stokes Croft but on that evening we were forestalled so it was decided to visit the same establishment the following evening when another club held its meetings.

We joined and were at once elected onto the organising committee and, after some period had elapsed, we said we would be interested in doing something ourselves. From that moment and for fifty years, Barbara and I organised hundreds of events for the three clubs of which we were members.

The one club we initially intended to join but didn't do so for 15 years celebrated its 100th anniversary in June 2011. Not many motoring clubs can boast that length of time with all its ups and downs. Nor can many motor clubs boast they started an interest in an international motor racing circuit way back in 1945 and to which thousands of people visit every year. It is universally known and is in Northamptonshire. I refer here to Silverstone, which together with Spa, are in my opinion and that of many others, the finest motor race tracks in the world.

Just after the Second World War, people started getting interested in sport, any sport, and this applied to motor sport which in any case had had a fair following pre-war.

A design for a 500cc powered car was devised by Coopers. This was taken up by motor engineers countrywide, using motorcycle engines as the power source. They produced a variation of reasonably priced racing four wheeled machines.

The Bristol Motorcycle and Light Car Club members wasted little time in getting to grips with this new section of motor sport. Several machines were built in garages in and around Bristol and, once built, a place was needed to test and race them. As we had many disused aerodromes in the West Country, some bright spark came up with the idea to go to Northamptonshire where he knew of such an area that could be used. No permission was obtained from the then owner and all descended on this ex-WD area owned by one Lord Hesketh (sponsor of the Norton rotary racing engine).

On hearing the hubbub of motorcycle engines, Lord Hesketh arrived on the scene in high dudgeon wanting to know who was responsible. The diplomat of the party explained the situation and with words such as, "You will ask next time", Silverstone was born.

At this time Barbara and I were spectators but it didn't take us long to become more involved. We proved our worth by doing anything that needed doing. The only way to learn is hands on.

We could put our hands to any vacancy which arose and eventually Barbara became official lap scorer to international time keepers and I became Clerk of the Course of any event we chose to organise from club to international, 15 years with the Bristol Motorcycle Club, 25 years with Bristol Motorcycle and Light Car Club and 10 years with Bristol Phoenix Motorcycle Club.

Because two, three or four wheels do not mix, the one is always jealous of the other. The three wheel section is a totally separate body, but then they are all mad. I have never mastered the art of driving a side car machine although have owned several three wheelers, they have all been car type units.

Chapter 16

I now come to the reason for my research, which was to locate the sister I had lost some 72 years before. I write sister but since we have different fathers, she is a half-sister but as I don't believe in halves, I will treat her as a full relative.

From a photograph I had over many years, a scribbled pencil mark revealed the name Partrick which I thought was a misspelt Patrick so what I did was to visit Bristol Library looking at electoral records – census papers – and other papers and microfiche documents. I visited Bristol Records Office on the recommendation of the vicar of Henbury Church to find my grandmother's (maternal) maiden name was Petherham and the youngest child of several. I also found her parents' names and where they were married as I did of the male side of the family.

I went back to my local library and with much help trawled the internet. After travelling down many blind alleys we came upon the name Partrick with initials N L, then I knew I had struck gold.

In the Cullimore family, there are many branches and to tell the difference a second name is used. In my own branch a boy's name is used for both boys and girls but in some others girls' names are used in a similar context for boys.

In the particular matter I was researching, I knew at

the back of my mind I was on the right track. Information came upon the screen that N. L. Partrick was married in 1948 and her name was now Niemiec.

Below that information was a reference to the fact that they had emigrated to New Zealand, believing she had no relatives locally. She had always believed that I was the true son of my foster parents and that consequently she could "plough her own furrow", after all she had her own life to lead, and so I sympathise with her decision to move.

Most people will not understand how being discarded by a parent feels to a child. Resentment builds up and remains for the rest of one's life, added to the fact that those children were not conceived in a true marriage bed. I was fostered once but I now learn that Norah was fostered on four occasions.

Once again through the internet, I found an address in the town of Gisborne, North Island. This I noted, jumped up and rushed around telling everyone the news. On getting home I immediately wrote a letter to the address quoted, saying that if it was incorrect would the recipient pass it on.

Some five weeks later the library staff phoned and asked if I would come and read an email they had received. It was from my sister and she said, "Please contact me by phone, earliest" and giving her number.

As they are about 12 hours time lapse from England I waited until evening before making a call. However at 4pm the doorbell rang and I answered it. A lady was standing there and I said, "Yes, can I help you?" thinking she was one of my parish residents needing assistance. Her reply was one word, "Niemiec". I immediately said, "Come in!" and it turned out she was a friend of my sister who had lived in

New Zealand in the town of Gisborne in her younger days and now lived in Bristol, not far from me. Norah had, very sensibly, asked her friend to act as a go-between to begin with.

I then made contact with my sister Norah herself. Since the initial contact, we have been writing and speaking on the phone and when I learnt of her trauma of being fostered so many times, I was livid. Had I known of the situation when she was living so close to us at the end of the war, there might have been a different outcome.

Now I have found my sister, I am overjoyed and she has expressed a similar feeling of me. I arranged to fly out to see her and her family, remake our acquaintance and see her husband. He fought with a Polish contingent in Italy during the Second World War and was in a prisoner-of -war camp.

I have now made a family tree dating from 1800 and, with more research, hope I can get back to the 1700s and see if they too were farmers.

Chapter 17

It was not until I was 17 in 1938 and my foster father had just died in Bristol Infirmary that I was given two pieces of paper which showed I was not who I thought I was. For all those years I had been of the impression that my birth grandmother was Aunt Mary and the little bundle in the shawl was a cousin. Now I knew differently and in a flash I realized I must have a half sister. I hadn't seen her for quite a long time, she was still a young girl then and by the time we were both old enough to discuss such things, the war had separated us.

Her childhood was a series of events from which she would have to pick herself up, dust herself down and carry on growing up. It is what has made her so self sufficient.

Mostly she lived with Grandmama in rented rooms only a mile and a half from us. Our birth mother went into service in a mansion somewhere. Through a twist of fate, our mother returned briefly to the rented rooms after being injured through a landmine landing on the mansion in which she was working as a cook.

After the war, Norah went back to live with Grandmama for, as she said just recently, "No one would have me".

At 18, Norah joined The Army and later met Boleslaw Niemiec, a Polish soldier, at a dance in Salisbury. It must have been a whirlwind union for they married in Bristol Pro-Cathedral when Norah was 20 and he was 25.

They had two sons, Robert and Stephen, and five years after the births moved to New Zealand to make Gisborne their home. A daughter, Marisa, was born in their new country.

My sister is a very strong-willed person – she has had to be to survive. We are both of a similar disposition and during my recent visit to her I was occasionally told off for doing something with which she did not agree.

She has made dozens of friends and even more acquaintances. The phones, and there are many in the house, ring for attention all day long, either it's the family keeping in touch or a friend with an invitation to dinner or another asking a favour. She is a very busy and caring person. I can't speak highly enough of her. She follows Grandmama in sheer determination, as I do. Generally she is up at 6.30am to look after her husband who is not well.

I always wondered where the family of Cullimores originated. For a long time, I had been searching churchyards in the Thornbury and Hill areas but on going to Bristol Records Office and searching, I found they had owned land at Hallen, near the city.

George Leonard Cullimore, our grandfather, married Mary Anne Petherham of Crooks Marsh, the youngest daughter of William and Sarah Petherham. George Leonard was somewhat older than Mary Anne. Heart problems seem to be hereditary in our family for he died in 1909 aged 69, their son died aged 40, Grandmama also died with heart problems aged 85 as did our mother, a year later in 1949 aged 60.

Chapter 18

This chapter includes extracts from an article published in the New Zealand Gisborne Herald on December 23rd 1995 and relates to my brother-in-law. I was so impressed by his fortitude that I felt I had to quote this article.

Boleslaw Niemiec was born in Boryslaw, an oil town in South East Poland, in September 1922. When he was two years of age, his mother died giving birth to her second child. His father, who was an oil driller for an American company, died some two years later of TB. As is usual in Poland, the family rallied around and he was brought up by one or another of his father's four sisters. Although they were poor, he was well cared for. Community help eased the load of feeding. The school provided a cup of cocoa and a bun in the morning and the town council supplied a meal in the afternoon for the needy.

Thanks to caring teachers who saw the potential in him, he started a three-year electrical apprenticeship at the age of 14. Two and a half years later, on September 1st 1939, Germany invaded Poland from the West, the Soviet Union then invaded from The East and in the ensuing partition, the Boryslaw area came under Soviet control.

Soon Soviet soldiers were arresting Poles on the slightest pretext and herding them on to trains bound East. Boleslaw and a friend were sickened by what they saw and, inspired by patriotism, resolved to join the escaped Polish forces who were regrouping in France.

Their plan was to walk 100 kilometres South to Hungary and make their way over the border but just 30 kilometres short of this boundary, they were caught by a Soviet border patrol with dogs. They were taken to the then Polish town of Lvov and interrogated over the following week. The Russians felt these Poles would fight for their country and so were enemies of Russia.

They were sent by railway cattle wagons to Kiev for trial, were advised to plead guilty to the charge of trying to escape to enemy territories, and were given 10-year sentences, incarcerated in Camp 22 in 19 Kolona (area) in Eastern Siberia.

As you may be aware, Poles are often of the Roman Catholic faith and celebration of Mass was forbidden but the Catholic prisoners gave a Latvian priest a crust of their black bread to bless and he returned it as the Eucharist. After three weeks in a filthy jail in Kiev, they boarded a train in January 1940 for their Trans-Siberian journey, packed 70 to a truck and locked inside for three days before they even left the station.

For nearly four weeks they trundled Eastwards. The food consisted of hot water and 200 grams of black bread in the morning and a small amount of soup at night. A bucket was filled with water for drinking. Another bucket was the latrine for the 70 people, with straw the only method of wiping. They had to adapt to these degrading conditions or become a mental vegetable.

The train stopped just East of Bratsk and North of central Mongolia and about 3,000 prisoners were decanted. Each received heavy cotton trousers, a jacket, gloves and a blanket for the 2,000 kilometre walk they were about to start.

Temperatures ranged from minus 20 to minus 40 degrees. They walked along the frozen Lena river whose ice was covered in a metre of snow. It was estimated that the column of prisoners stretched five kilometres. Those at the front had the hardest job to get through that snow. Even fit men died under such conditions. Hunger, cold and fatigue did for many.

"Bob" Niemiec, for that is what I will call him as it is the style by which he is now known, listened to the advice of cold weather experts, which was "Rub your hands, your nose and your ears with snow to keep the blood flowing".

To augment the meagre food rations, he ate tree bark and even his boot laces. He gave himself every chance but believed his survival was due to a much higher power than his own. He still believes that today. He prayed constantly and is convinced he was guided by God, which is why he has such a strong faith. Many a time he could have given up for it was so hard to stay alive. Again and again he felt he was being looked after.

After seven weeks heading North East, the marchers reached their destination, a camp five kilometres past Ya-kutsk in Eastern Siberia. No-one knew how many had died on the trek. The camp at which they arrived was already thousands strong, with hundreds of huts containing Lat-vians, Estonians, Finns, Ukrainians and Russians from all walks of life. Some had been there for 15 or even 20 years.

After a respite of two days, the newcomers started work. Bob was in a six-man team tree felling. Because he was so weak, he was given the task of trimming branches from the felled trees. Productivity was a life or death struggle. Every gang had to produce two neatly stacked piles, each containing 8cubic metres of railway sleepers. If this wasn't produced, the food ration dropped from 300 grams to 200 grams or even 100 grams, so in the end prisoners could get weaker and weaker until they died.

Summer transformed the frozen wastes into mud and slush, mosquitoes and sand flies emerged but there was at least the opportunity to pick up wild berries and edible grasses. Lack of vitamins caused a condition of night blind-ness which could generally be cured by a course of cod liver oil and Bob needed it on several occasions.

In July 1941 Germany attacked the Soviet Union and everyone in the camp was urged to increase production. About 700 prisoners were told they would earn reduced sentences by producing something for the Soviets in an-other place. Bob happened to be in that group as he had electrical knowledge but his friend was left in the camp and lost to the world.

The seven-week journey was as bad as the first trek but by now Bob was determined to escape. About five days into the train journey to Novosibrisk, North West of Mongolia, Bob felt this would be his last chance. He volunteered to empty the latrine bucket and then hid underneath the train. No-one missed him so he scuffled to another train and stole the uniform of a Soviet soldier who had gone to sleep in his underclothes. Wearing the uniform and using the money and ration book in it, he stayed in the area for a few days getting his bearings.

He picked up casual work in a market with food as payment and visited the town library seeking information to get himself across the border. His spoken Russian was passable but he had to be careful. He found a map in the library and, after making notes of train timetables, he posed as a refugee and moved West towards the Caspian Sea. Rail travel posed few problems as the carriages were full of refugees.

He walked 200 kilometres down the Eastern shore of the Caspian Sea but signs warning of land mines stopped him 20 metres short of Iran. He had to retrace his steps to Krasnovodsk to catch the ferry to Baku on the other side of the Caspian. He got work in bazaars and restaurants for the fare to Tbilisi, having discarded his Russian uniform (a wise move).

He found himself in Azerbaijan where the local people were hostile to the Russians. He found work in a restaurant and was befriended by an Azerbaijan family who agreed to take him across the border into Turkey. After climbing mountains and crossing streams for four days, he collapsed in an exhausted state on the Turkish side of the border where he was found by police.

Bob was in hospital with double pneumonia for six weeks and unconscious for the first two. The British Embassy arranged paperwork and, once fit, he boarded a Turkish steamer in Istanbul to Alexandria in Egypt where he was met by Polish forces.

Sent to Tobruk as part of the Polish artillery, he soon learned to drive a varied assortment of vehicles. After the relief of Tobruk, he was sent to Northern Iraq and Iran to help pick up Polish nationals given amnesty by the Soviet Union to fight the Germans. After being deprived of proper food for so long, many could not manage the rations now offered and thousands died of dysentery.

For four months, Bob drove anything on wheels in the deserts of Iraq, including tanks. In 1943 he was trained as one of 32 signallers in the Polish Fifth Division Second Battalion and reached a speed of 120 Morse Code symbols a minute but just before the invasion of Italy, he was transferred to the Polish Second Armoured Division, a move that certainly saved his life.

In May 1944, the Fifth Division took part in the fierce fighting at Monte Cassino and not a single member of Bob's old signals team survived. The Second Armoured Division took Monte Cassino to the North and Bob, driving a tank, hit a mine suffering a minor injury. His war finished in Udine, North Eastern Italy, but it was November 1946 before he arrived in Britain where he sought a new life.

At a dance in Salisbury, he met my sister who was an ATS clerk. She thought he was a bit forward to hold her hand without an introduction but he hardly knew any English. However, after a whirlwind courtship (he was very handsome in his young days, in spite of the privations he had suffered) they married, after some pressure from our mother at the Pro-Cathedral in Bristol in 1948. Norah helped him to learn to speak English but when excited he still lapses into his native tongue.

Because of his wartime experiences, it was counted as the completion of his apprenticeship and in 1953 he and my sister emigrated to New Zealand with their sons, Robert and Stephen. They did so on a whim, as both our Grandmama and mother had died from heart conditions and my sister knew nothing of our relationship, we both having been brought up in separate households.

I knew of her relationship to me but she knew nothing of me, always of the understanding that I was the true son of my foster parents.

In an aside to Bob's exploits during the war, I read an interesting article of which he was also aware. Wojtek was a Syrian brown bear who was adopted by the Polish 2nd Corps in 1941. He had been rescued by a child as an orphan and the child later exchanged the bear for food.

Wojtek acted as the soldiers did and thought it was human. It lived in an Army tent, was trained to salute when addressed and in 1944 at Monte Cassino took shells to gun emplacements as would a soldier. When the Poles returned to Britain, it lived on a farm in Berwickshire for a period but after the Poles left it was put into Edinburgh Zoo where it died aged 22 in 1962.

Chapter 19

My trip to New Zealand to see my sister after so many years was very exciting. Although I had been involved in research on aeroplane manufacture, I had never flown before. When I arrived at Gisborne Airport, my sister was waiting for me with a whole tribe of family and friends plus a photographer and reporter from the local Gisborne Herald newspaper who wished to write about our long lost lives and our meeting again after 72 years apart.

It was strange that after my wife and I had been on our own for so many years that I should find 11 relations whom I had not realized existed – my sister, her husband and children and grandchildren. Three I have yet to meet still but am expecting them to call on me some time this year, Stephen to return to his birth city of Bristol with his partner and children.

I also met some other wonderful, generous people in the two months I was away and saw some extraordinary scenery. I hope I will return but that will depend on the Good Lord.

Speaking of the Good Lord leads me to write, "Faith is everything" and had it not been for Bob's faith, he would not be here today. But faith is faith no matter in what form this happens to be and there are many in this world. Both the Cullimores and Petherham families have been staunch C of E supporters over the last 210 years so it surprised me that my sister had converted to Roman Catholicism. I can understand that, as her husband is of Polish origin and he follows his mother country's disposition to the RC faith.

My foster father and some of his sisters were placed in a similar situation when their local holy fathers decreed they were not married because of dissimilar religious beliefs and as a consequence their children were illegitimate.

When I travelled to New Zealand to visit my extended family, I was invited to attend a rededication of the church, St Mary Star of the Sea, Gisborne, on January 1st 2012. I was in New Zealand to gain new experiences and this certainly was one. The whole service was conducted in the Maori language.

The eucharist to me means the same in any church, so on our second visit I presented myself to receive communion. The priest spoke to my sister after the service and came to dinner on the following Wednesday evening. I was advised he might wish to speak to me so I prepared myself.

During the meal he advised me that I should not have taken communion at his service as I was not of his religious persuasion. I had guessed this question might arise so I related to him the experience of my father and his sisters. His reply was that the comment should never have been made and would I consider trading my allegiance.

My reply was that, not to embarrass my sister and her husband, I would speak with him when he was leaving to get into his car. Taking communion is a representative act irrespective of the brand of faith, it is a faith in itself. Whether the body of Christ is represented by a wafer, a bagel or a stale piece of bread, and his blood represented by red wine or other liquid, it is a representation only and it is the belief only that matters.

I imagine from his attitude that he went away to consult the rules once again. The following week I visited an Anglican church and took communion there with no comment. When I returned to England I attended my own church some 20 miles from where I now live and again received communion with no comment. I say my church for I have attended there for over 85 years ever since I was six years of age and admitted to the choir.

Small changes have been made as to any building over such a long period but the pews, choir stalls and organ are the same and although the congregation is smaller than in my early years and mainly of the white-haired variety, it is nevertheless my church.

Chapter 20

On my trip to New Zealand, the first place I was taken to was the memorial to Captain James Cook who met the Maoris on what is now Gisborne beach in October 1769. Also there was the figure of a young lad called Nicholas Young who was the first to see land from The Endeavour. The land he sighted is now named Young Nick's Head.

Many Gisborne streets are named after 19th century British statesmen such as Grey, Peel, Gladstone, Palmerston and Disraeli. The HB Williams Memorial Library is a vast place. Williams was a descendant of Gisborne's first missionary. The library is fronted by a stained glass window which spans the whole of the building. Unveiled in 1993, it depicts the flow of time in Gisborne/Tairawhiti from its volcanic past to the present day. Central to the work is the Toka-a-Taiau, a rock that delineates the boundary between the Ngati Porou and Rongowhakaata tribes and on the same rock Captain Cook first met with the Tangata Whenua in 1769. I also discovered that Gisborne is the first city in the world to see the light of a new day.

Standing on the riverbank and on the harbour complex is the Marina Restaurant, once the ballroom of a large house, where I was taken with my sister as a surprise by one of her many friends, a teacher originally from Shropshire.

As I sat at the table, I was immediately struck by the impressive manner in which the table was laid. My foster parents had for many years been in the hotel business and on entering any food establishment I judge it by the staff's actions. I was not surprised to find that the food was also excellent.

The harbour, formed in the 1920s, held many boats and I took advantage of my nephew's generosity to board one for a trip to the cliffs of Young Nick's Head.

In another memorable eating experience I was taken to the SA building, the New Zealand Forces restaurant, where for a pittance you can have a drink and eat a good meal in the company of nice people.

Chapter 21

My sister knew the famous Westonbirt Arboretum in Gloucestershire from being brought up in Bristol and wanted to show me that New Zealand wasn't to be outdone. She took me to the National Arboretum of New Zealand at Eastwood Hill, some 35 kilometres North West of Gisborne and 30 minutes drive through the picturesque Ngatapa Valley. The valley is a very productive area growing oranges, lemons, grapes, Indian corn and cabbages.

On arrival, it was explained that I couldn't walk far, so out came a four-wheel drive Suzuki to drive us over the vast area of trees and shrubs.

The aims of the arboretum are:

1 To protect and enhance the collection established by Douglas Cook.

2 To maintain Eastwood Hill as the most comprehensive collection of wood plant material in New Zealand.

3 To conserve and promote the conservation of rare and endangered plants.

4 To assist visitors in understanding the beauty and complexity of the plant world

5 To promote understanding of the world flora especially in regard to cool and warm temperate trees.

Douglas Cook (1884-1967) was the founder of Eastwood Hill in its present form. He started farming here in 1910, was wounded in World War I and recuperated in Britain where he was so impressed by the beautiful gardens and parks that he decided on his return to New Zealand to create one of his own. By the time of his death he had spent £55,000 on sourcing 5,000 different types of trees and shrubs from all over the world. In 1965 Eastwood was sold to Bill Williams and in 1975 it became a trust.

Our journey by four-wheel drive took an hour and we had an excellent commentary from our driver.

Chapter 22

One of the highlights was a ride on a restored steam locomotive, an 1897 WA Class 2-6-2T built in Dunedin and worked out of Gisborne from 1911 to 1942. Today it is the sole survivor of 11 of its class.

Our journey took us South for 15 miles into the Wharerata Forest but first it must cross an airfield, the only train to do so, with notification that it is so doing being sent to the airport authorities first. It crosses the wide plain on which Gisborne City lies, then climbs to 1,500 feet among mountains rising a further 600 to 750 feet. The track balances on a ledge just wide enough for the one track with a loop on a plateau for changing the engine from front to rear.

Building this railway was a remarkable achievement, starting in 1929 from both the Gisborne and Waikokopu ends. All work stopped in 1931 because of the Depression and restarted in 1936. Thirteen tunnels were built. One night floods swept away the single men's quarters of No. 4 Camp at Kopuawhara with the loss of 22 lives. A monument was erected to them along the route.

The Waikura Tunnel at 1,443 metres long was pierced on May 12th 1939 with a margin of error of only 22mm in the width and 18mm in the height. The Tikiwhata tunnel is 2,989 metres long and was completed in late 1941. The Kopuawhara Viaduct was completed in July 1942 and is 162 metres long and 39 metres high. The bridge spanning the Waipaoa River at 329 metres has had to be lengthened twice because of the unstable river banks.

Since returning to England, I have learned that because of a torrential rain storm, some of the track base has fallen into the South Pacific so no services can operate for now. Whether the volunteers can ever afford to make repairs is anyone's guess as the expense would be so great.

Chapter 23

The three-day R&V Music Festival is held each New Year and is rather like the Glastonbury festival. It attracted about 30,000 people this year from all over both the North and South Islands and Australia.

I heard all about it from a group of five lads, headed by one of my sister's grandsons, who came to dinner one evening, had showers and changed their clothes and then headed back to their tents. My sister was cooking all day, hoping all the food would be consumed by hungry mouths, and it was.

To get home, thousands of festival-goers had to negotiate the Waioeka Gorge, which terrifies many with its unstable land combined with rock falls in wet weather. Around midnight, a severe rock fall occurred and hit a car. Also a bridge was washed out and people who had driven some 100 miles had to turn around and drive back to Gisborne and then go round the East Cape coast road some 300 miles. The fuel stations were packed with vehicles running low on petrol.

The road staff worked all night and by the following lunchtime the route was open but only in one direction. My sister's grandson and his friend had to take the long way round and arrived back 24 hours after setting out. He then had to go straight to work two hours later.

Chapter 24

Having been the Mayor of my Borough and Chairman of my Unitary Authority, I was invited to meet the Mayor of Gisborne District Council for tea. He and his family are friends of my sister. Mr Foon is of Chinese extraction and went to school with my niece Marisa. He is a very pleasant person and has a very retentive memory. Whilst having tea, he was still conducting council business on the phone and on reading the evening paper, checked that the reporter had written word-for-word what had been said.

Earlier he had been on a fishing trip (6am) and been violently seasick, giving his breakfast to the fishes, and wanted to cancel our meeting but because we were already in situ, he agreed to meet us and we had an interesting afternoon, discussing politics and council composition.

Although all Gisborne Councillors are independent, he supported the views of Mr Cameron. On this particular day, I was wearing a red tie and a blue shirt, which made him ask to which party I belonged. I just pointed to my shirt.

My sister felt that before I left I should see more of the country so she arranged for her husband, who is not a well person, to go into a rest home for five days while we travelled to some places I wished to see.

There are only two ways to travel overland in New Zealand, by air or road. The major coast roads are excellent but those that cross the mountains are nothing but bend after bend.

In most countries, one judges travel by distance but here one does it by time taken. The roads are rarely straight, especially those we travelled on, with every corner marked by black arrows on a yellow background with an indication as to its severity.

On this journey from Gisborne through the mountain pass of Waioeka to the North West Coast and the town of Rotorua, where we stayed for two nights, the road passes through flat land for some 70 kilometres, where food is grown and cattle reared. Then at a small town named Matawai we started climbing into the mountains and to the head of the Waioeka Gorge. To the West is wilderness and the Te Urewera National Park. I wanted to see if the fears people had of this route, of which I had heard, were justified. Going downhill for an awfully long way, we came upon rest areas very nicely designed with commemorative plaques.

I realized that some people's fears were justified as in parts we travelled over road surfaces which were only sticking to the river banks by good will and would in the short term have to be supported by gabions - blocks of stone encased in wire mesh - from the river bed and built about 60ft high.

From the start of the gorge to Waioeka Pa is about 40 kilometres, an extremely interesting journey. Any minute one expects to fall into the river bed. But then we came to flat land where once again were sheep, cattle and acres and acres of woodland. Timber lorries were pounding up and down the gorge in a hurry to be unloaded in Gisborne and go back for a further load.

We by-passed the large town of Opotiki and travelled on to Rotorua where we booked into a motel. We went to see the hot springs which are fed from Lake Rotorua, heated underground then rising to the surface as steam causing the water to be boiling hot. So dangerous is it that the area is fenced off with warning notices but these failed to prevent several deaths. Hydrogen sulphide emanates from these areas causing bad smells which people seem able to ignore.

This is a very volcanic area close to the moving plates of the Earth's crust, the mountains formed by this movement millions of years ago. Large hills have been formed of sea sediment in strata. The only flat land is near the oceans and is well used for crops and animal rearing, including Aberdeen Angus and Hereford cattle. I even saw a rare herd of

Old English. Sheep are raised on the steeper slopes because they are more agile. I wanted to see Lake Taupo, a very large lake sitting in a volcanic crater 25 kilometres x 30 kilometres.

On our third day, we decided to return home. We could have gone a different way, from Taupo over the Ahimanawa and Maungaharuru Ranges but chose the part we knew. Overnight rain had brought down boulders and the Highways Department were out in great strength on three falls as traffic waited for the obstructions to be removed.

I have since learned of a massive land slip of some 200,000 cubic metres which has completely blocked both the roadway and river bed. Some attempt has been made to get traffic through on a one-way system but it will certainly take a lot of large earth moving equipment and much time to rectify the problem. There will also be concern as to whether the roadway is still intact.

This landslide is costing local businesses a lot of money as the transport now has to go a further 300 miles around the coast road to and from Gisborne. It must be of national concern and I am sure the Wellington Parliament is giving it much discussion and attention.

Further landslides on the Gisborne to Napier rail line have caused more upset as now all rail traffic has ceased and the National Government appears to be unable to fund the repairs running into millions of New Zealand dollars.

My holiday was rapidly coming to a close. I had met my extended family, with one exception, that of Stephen, my sister's middle child, who lives in Australia. I write child but he is of course a grown man with a daughter of 12. I hope he will be able to come to Bristol this year.

I met some remarkable people during my stay. It meant

a great deal to me to see my long-lost sister after so many years and to meet her husband and their family. I received a very warm welcome. To my astonishment, I found that on leaving in a little 20-seater plane from Gisborne Airport to Kuala Lumpur, quite a crowd arrived to see me off. So emotional was it all that I left my raincoat in the lounge and had to hold up the plane's departure while I went back for it.

Shall I make the journey again? If I am spared and I feel as well as I do today, I will be heading back again in two years.

Epilogue

On the female side of my blood family, the names have changed many times over the years since 1800 – Petherham, Cullimore, Partrick, Niemiec, Bramwell. The Petherhams married into the Cullimore family but our particular branch has died out.

When I was quite young, I decided there were too many people in this world and that if I married, the union would not produce any children. As it so happened, I married a lovely girl who unfortunately had suffered such traumas in being born herself, leading to life-long effects, that she was also of the same mind. So we saw to it that children were not for us.

When I leave this mortal coil, I wonder if anyone will tend the many graves which I have cared for over the years?

Thinking about my life, I realize one has to have a passion to achieve anything. This is certainly true of my marriage, my sporting years and my political period. The latter started in my youth but only developed later in my life when I seemed to have more time available (my sporting years were coming to an end) with the help of a devoted wife who had similar views to my own, thank goodness.

Behind every good man there is a better woman doing the pushing, whether for her sake or her man's is debatable but I have seen it time and again. My own situation was no different and I am so very glad to have noticed a young girl in an office window to whom I was attracted.

Had they lived long enough to see the end product, I believe both my foster parents, Thomas and Mary Sarah, would have been proud of their daughter-in-law.

Now I am left alone I find it somewhat wearing having no-one to banter with, exchange serious views or have an argument but I do make visits to the graves of Thomas, Mary Sarah and Barbara where I can commune with those who have been my life.

I also visit my blood family graves as, other than myself, there is no-one handy to pay them any attention and I report back to my sister whenever I have made a visit.

How good it feels to have found her again!

Family Tree

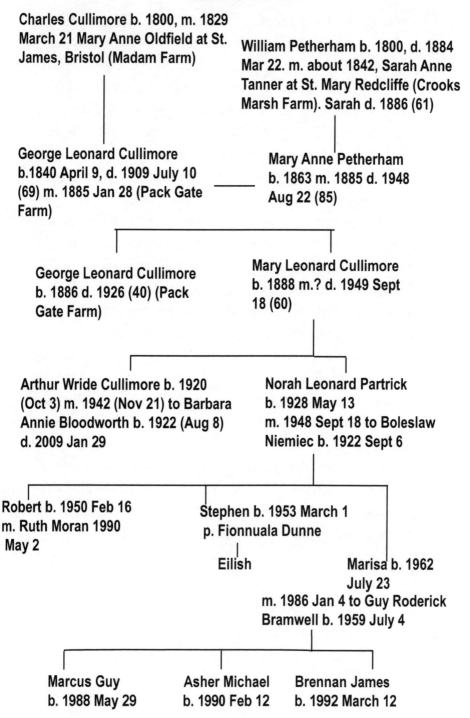

Charles Cullimore b. 1800, m. 1829 March 21 Mary Anne Oldfield at St. James, Bristol (Madam Farm)

William Petherham b. 1800, d. 1884 Mar 22. m. about 1842, Sarah Anne Tanner at St. Mary Redcliffe (Crooks Marsh Farm). Sarah d. 1886 (61)

George Leonard Cullimore b.1840 April 9, d. 1909 July 10 (69) m. 1885 Jan 28 (Pack Gate Farm)

Mary Anne Petherham b. 1863 m. 1885 d. 1948 Aug 22 (85)

George Leonard Cullimore b. 1886 d. 1926 (40) (Pack Gate Farm)

Mary Leonard Cullimore b. 1888 m.? d. 1949 Sept 18 (60)

Arthur Wride Cullimore b. 1920 (Oct 3) m. 1942 (Nov 21) to Barbara Annie Bloodworth b. 1922 (Aug 8) d. 2009 Jan 29

Norah Leonard Partrick b. 1928 May 13 m. 1948 Sept 18 to Boleslaw Niemiec b. 1922 Sept 6

Robert b. 1950 Feb 16 m. Ruth Moran 1990 May 2

Stephen b. 1953 March 1 p. Fionnuala Dunne

Eilish

Marisa b. 1962 July 23 m. 1986 Jan 4 to Guy Roderick Bramwell b. 1959 July 4

Marcus Guy b. 1988 May 29

Asher Michael b. 1990 Feb 12

Brennan James b. 1992 March 12